Happy Birth

Love Betsy

Pugs

Illustrated by Jenny MacKendrick

The History Press

First published 2015

The History Press
The Mill, Brimscombe Port
Stroud, Gloucestershire, GL5 2QG
www.thehistorypress.co.uk

British Library Cataloguing in Publication Data.
A catalogue record for this book is available from the
British Library.

ISBN 978 0 7509 6399 2

Design by The History Press
Printed in China

Pugs ...

are lovers, not fighters.

They make great family dogs ...

and come in two different colours.

But they all have the same inquisitive
temperament,

exuberant nature

and waggy rear end.

They're great entertainers –

especially when they sit like Buddha.

Pugs like ...

eating

almost anything.

Sometimes it gets out of hand

and sometimes it gets stuck in the most
annoying places.

They don't mind helping themselves

but they'd rather it came on a plate.

Pugs like routine

especially when it involves food

or sleep

or both.

They love to nap ...

in the strangest places

and in the strangest positions,

but mostly wherever it's warm.

Pugs need ...

a lot of maintenance,

a lot of attention

and a lot of tissues

(for both ends).

They need to be near you

whether you want them or not.

They need a lot of house training ...

it may be years before they get it right.

Pugs need a lot of wiggle room,

a lot of diversion,

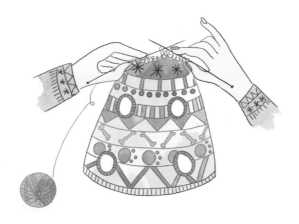

an owner who'll spoil them

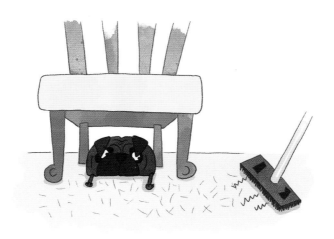

and a reliable hoover.

Pugs don't like ...

being alone,

being told what to do

or being shouted at

(unless it's dinner time).

They don't like rain

AT ALL.

They get bored with training

unless you make it really fun.

Pugs are ...

small and sturdy,

very cute,

energetic as puppies ...

and lazy as adults.

They are manipulative,

vocal,

bossy,

easily distracted,

jealous,

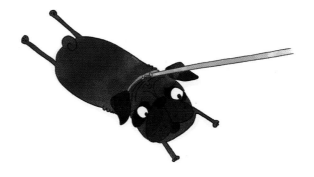

and stubborn ...

but we still love them

even if they are very persistent lap dogs.

Pugs have ...

hypnotic eyes,

drooly mouths,

wrinkly skin,

massive tongues,

snotty noses

and snotty bums.

They have no sense of shame ...

and no sense of personal space.

Pugs will ...

never catch anything

except a cold.

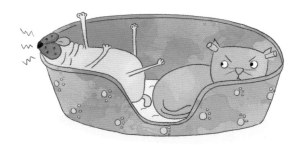

They'll snore

and fart

and make silly faces,

get under your feet,

under your skin

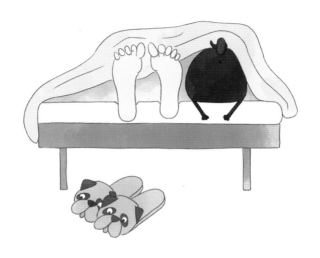

and under your covers.

They'll play the fool,

never grow up,

make you laugh

and make you cry.

But mostly they'll bring you joy ...

and a lifetime of love.

About the Illustrator

Jenny MacKendrick studied drawing and applied arts at the University of the West of England. She now works as an artist and illustrator from her studio in Bristol, which she shares with Shona, her large and hairy Hungarian Wirehaired Vizsla, who is often to be found hiding under the desk.

Also in this Series
Border Terriers
Labradors
Springer Spaniels

www.thehistorypress.co.uk